Tony Hawks is a radio and TV comedian who makes regular appearances on *I'm Sorry I Haven't a Clue* and *Just a Minute*, and not so regular appearances on *Have I Got News for You* and *QI* (despite having repeatedly made it clear that he is available). His six books include the *Sunday Times* bestselling *Round Ireland with a Fridge*, *Playing the Moldovans at Tennis* and *Once Upon a Time in the West...Country*. He is the same height as Tony Hawk.

The A to Z of
Skateboarding

First published in 2019

Unbound
6th Floor Mutual House, 70 Conduit Street, London W1S 2GF
www.unbound.com
All rights reserved

While every effort has been made to trace the owners of copyright material reproduced
herein, the publisher would like to apologise for any omissions and will be pleased to incorporate
missing acknowledgements in any further editions.

Skateboarding facts courtesy of www.skatereview.com,
www.dissentskateshop.com and www.brandongaille.com

'Tony Hawk' biography courtesy of https://en.wikipedia.org/wiki/Dylan_Thomas

Text Design by PDQ

A CIP record for this book is available from the British Library

ISBN 978-1-78352-672-7 (hardback)
ISBN 978-1-78352-674-1 (ebook)

Printed in Slovenia by DZS Grafik

1 3 5 7 9 8 6 4 2

The A to Z of
Skateboarding

TONY HAWKS

unbound

My name is Tony Hawks. I am an English comedian and author. I am not a bad bloke. I've been convicted of no offences, I pay my tax and the only real blot on my moral copybook is once suggesting that the world might be a better place if Chris de Burgh split up. And yet it seems that I have been singled out to be tortured each week by a host of ill-informed and poorly educated young people who write to me thinking that I am the American skateboarder Tony Hawk. Now, I realise that they're simply making a mistake, and I fully accept that people make mistakes in life. (I've done it. I once believed that Tony Blair was principled, honest and a good prime minister.) However, the only way these kids can get these emails to me is by visiting my website, www.tony-hawks.com, and then clicking on the contact button. This is the point at which the mistake starts to nudge towards gross stupidity. Anyone looking at my site would know within seconds that I am not a professional skateboarder, and they might think again before firing off an email asking how to do a '900' or an 'ollie'. However, American youth proceed with their irritating emails, making my life unbearable and driving me to despair.

A few years ago I decided to fight back. I began replying to these emails. My tone was acerbic. I was unforgiving of grammatical errors and spelling. I was harsh. Some might say cruel. But for me it was survival. Either I fought back, or I went down under a barrage of mindless mails telling me how gr8 I was. It was a gr8ness that would, if left unchecked, inevitably result in my mental breakdown. So: what is contained in this book is my attempt at self-therapy. It's an outlet for me, a chance for me to vent my feelings of frustration. Yes, at times I turn on the entire skateboarding community and that's probably unfair – but I had to do it. It was a case of sink or swim. Skateboarding was not an option.

I hope you enjoy what you read on the following pages. In their philosophical work of genius 'Ebony and Ivory', Stevie Wonder and Paul McCartney refer to the fact that there's good and bad in everyone. Maybe that's true. If it is, then in the pages ahead I appeal to the badness in you. Please laugh at what is, essentially, a fifty-something, well-educated bloke mercilessly taking the piss out of a bunch of enthusiastic kids. Feel no guilt. Allowing an outlet for this rather unpleasant side of yourself will mean that you are less likely to embarrass yourself, when out in your car, by shouting and making gestures at other drivers who make minor mistakes.

I expect no awards for this book.* I simply want closure; primarily of skateboard parks. If you don't like what you read, then I suggest you send an email of complaint to Tony Hawk, the skateboarder.

Now fuck off and get reading.

---

* Not unless they introduce the Gratuitous Humiliation of Children award.

© Ben Hunt

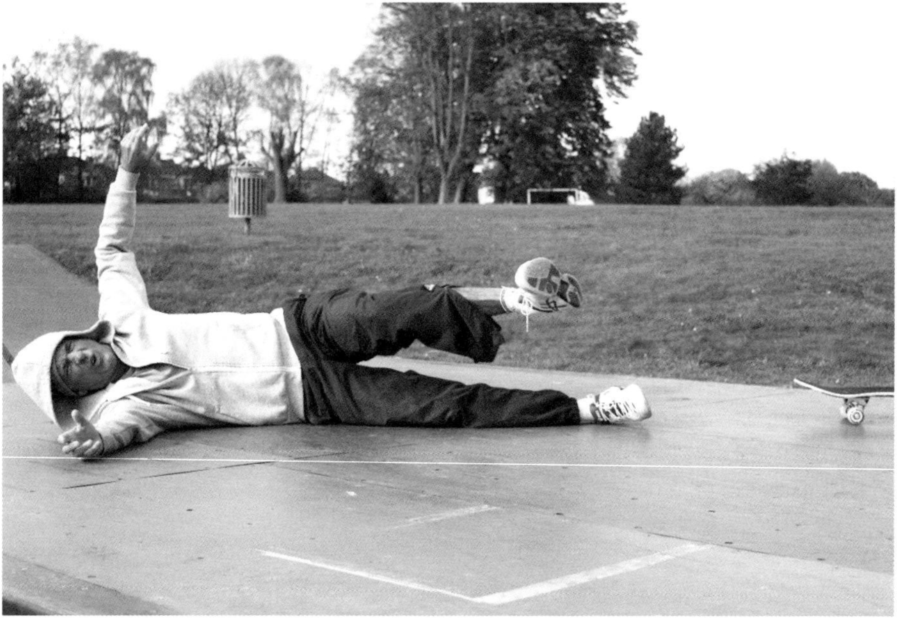

Arse

(Or ass, if you're unfortunate enough to be American)

The arse is situated at the bottom, or 'arse-end', of our bodies. The arse is what you tend to fall on when you go skateboarding – although it is not exclusively the body part on which one lands (see entry E). Opposite is a photo of a handsome man falling on his arse. Ouch.

Abusing your arse like this can be avoided in a number of ways, the best of which, unquestionably, is simply not to go skateboarding (see entry N). It's quite unnecessary.

A man falling on his arse skiing.

However, if for some reason reading quietly and studying grammar is not enough to bring pleasure and you have to do something stupid, then go skiing.

You will note a key difference between the skier and the skateboarder. One falls on snow, the other on tarmac. Snow is soft, tarmac is hard. The skier is happy-go-lucky, the skateboarder stupid.

DEAR TONY HAWK I LIKE SKATEBOARDING TO. I THINK YOUR AWESOME. I HAVE A BOOK OF YOU AT THE X-GAMES. I WISH I HAD A AUDAGRAPH OF YOU BECAUSE YOU ARE COOL. WHEN I GROW UP I WANT TO LIVE IN BEVERLY HILLS.

FROM AUSTIN

Dear Austin,

You can have my Audagraph just as soon as we can get it fixed and running properly. As you will be aware, the Audagraph is a complex piece of machinery and needs constant oiling and I'm afraid that I have been rather remiss with this of late. As for your ambition to 'live in Beverly Hills' when you grow up, I urge you to begin the growing-up process forthwith.

TH

FACT: Skateboarding was invented in the late 1940s.

THE WORLD WAS STILL REELING FROM TWO WORLD WARS THAT ROCKED THE VERY FOUNDATIONS OF HUMANITY. THE DOOR WAS OPEN FOR A BLOODY SILLY PASTIME.

hey darlin y do u tink ur so gd?

u not!

av seen so many ppl like u n ur all tink u own da place!

y do u make ur games so gd? shame bout da man bhind them!

rite bk soon ur biggest fans lewis n paddy

xXx

Goodness me. And you reckon you're my biggest fans? What do you write to people you don't like?

TH

10

These are the options.

Breakages

There is overwhelming evidence to show that you are far more likely to break a bone in your body by skateboarding than by doing something far more rewarding; like spreading peanut butter on a piece of bread, or even simply having a dump.

hi tony, i wear a thong to sk8 sometimes.. do you think it'll make me better? I'm ate years old. can you teach me a backflip? do you get lots of woman? i saw a boobie once. maybe we can sk8 sometimes, you could kinda show me the ways of being a man, and what to do with my manly.. my momy says i'll find out one day

bye, you're biggest fan in the whole world

shane

Shane

I'm no angel but I have standards. And one of them is not showing 'ate'-year-olds the ways of being a man, and what to do with their manlies. Sorry.

TH

FACT: The net worth of skateboarding is $4.8 billion in the market today.

MOST OF THIS MONEY IS GENERATED BY ANNOYING SKATEBOARDERS BEING PAID A DOLLAR TO 'GO AWAY'.

tony,

will you ever retire from skate boarding

where do you live

what is your favourite trick

your fan

Justin

Justin

? This is a question mark. Don't be afraid of it.

Now answers to your queries:

Will I ever retire from skateboarding?
Only when I can slide along on the thing without falling off and bashing my knee.

Where do I live?
Just outside Barnstaple.

What is my favourite trick?
The one where I pull the ace of spades out of my arse.

TH

ⓒ

Cup of tea

One of the worst aspects of skateboarding is what happens to your cup of tea while in transit. It is extraordinary just how much tea is lost to spillage. In 2010 alone, more than 3.75 million litres of tea were spilled (roughly equivalent to 750,000 cups) – and this was only in the Kettering area. The best way to ensure that you can drink your entire cup of tea without spilling anything is to stop skateboarding (see entry N).

Tony
How hard was it to do the 900?
Jed

Jed

Quite hard. Especially since around 750 of them said 'no' at first. I needed to be very persuasive.

TH

FACT: About 11 million people self-report that they enjoy skateboarding on a regular basis.

BUT THERE IS GOOD REASON TO SUSPECT THAT 10,999,998 OF THEM ARE LYING. THE OTHER TWO ARE CONCUSSED.

Hi Tony, I don't know if you'll read this message, and you probably get this 100 times a day, but when I was a kid in 4th grade, we could have wrote to any famous person. People wrote to eminem, kim kardashian, and I chose to write to you. I was the only one in my class to get a response, So thanks dude! Rich

Rich

How nice to be bothered by you on two separate occasions. Do you mind if we leave it here?

TH

A skateboarder who fancies himself quite a lot doing a trick.

Disappointment

This is what we all feel when a skateboarder shows us a new trick that they have been working on. On occasions we may attempt to show approval, but in most cases our underlying disdain will be palpable. Rather than issuing an insincere 'Well done' or 'That was good', far better to offer up the more genuine 'Why don't you stop skateboarding and do something meaningful with your time?' (See entry N.)

WILL FLORIDA BE INCLUDED IN ANY OF YOU TOURING EVENTS??

IF SO, WHICH CITIES.

THANKS WILLIE

Florida, no. Bexhill-on-Sea, yes. Any use to you?

TH

FACT: 77 per cent. That's the percentage of skateboarders who prefer to shop with small speciality brands rather than the top brand names that are on the market.

0.005 PER CENT. THAT'S THE PERCENTAGE OF THE REST OF US WHO GIVE A TOSS.

Zielig hoor, jezelf een beetje voordoen als Tony Hawk in die mailtjes. Volgens mij ben je gewoon gefrustreerd dat je Tony Hawks heet en niet Tony Hawk. Jij hebt zeker een indentiteitsprobleem. Sterkte ermee, en moge je ooit nog terecht komen in je eigen ego.

I think it's important that you know that I'm fluent in Dutch and I resent your comments. I have never on any occasion, even on special birthdays, worn matching mittens and corduroys. (Though don't think it hasn't been tempting.)

TH

A boy wearing both elbow pads and a gormless expression.

Elbow

When skateboarding, the elbows are particularly vulnerable to the hard surfaces upon which one is travelling. When falling occurs, as it invariably does, then the elbows come into contact with said hard surface, and pain is nearly always the direct consequence.

Intelligent skateboarders get around these problems by wearing elbow pads, as we see in the opposite photo.

However, the best (and cheapest) way to avoid elbow injuries is by not skateboarding at all (see entry N). Here is a list of other things you could do instead:

1. Make tea.
2. Drink tea.
3. Read this:

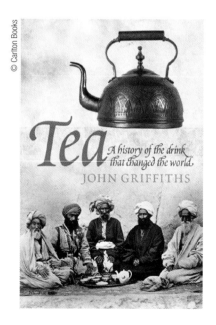

Dear Tony,

My nephew Nicky loves skateboarding but refuses to wear the safety equipment when he does it outside of the skateboarding parks. I would appreciate it if you let him know how important it is to wear the safety gear. He just turned 11 years old. I appreciate anything you can do to persuade him to be safe when he is skateboarding.

Sincerely,
Michele

Dear Michele,

It's always a good idea to wear a condom. I always do, certainly when I'm outside a skateboard park. I shall try to persuade your nephew to do so, but since I don't know who he is – or indeed where he is, it'll be tough. Fingers crossed though.

TH

Falling off

To some extent I have already covered this with my entries on arses and elbows.[*] But it's not guaranteed that you will always fall off your skateboard and land on your arse or elbow. You may fall off and land on your knees. However, pain prevention awaits in the form of knee pads, which are fitted in a similar manner to the elbow pads.

It may be that you fall off your skateboard in the manner shown opposite.

In this event, neither knee nor elbow pads are much help. Of course, our skater in this case is a drawing and will feel no pain. Which is a shame.

---

[*] Trust me, I know my arse from my elbow. For those skateboarders reading this who don't know, one is a Manchester-based alternative rock band, and the other is the thing that skateboarders mostly talk out of.

just wanted to say thanks for taking the time out to sign our son's skate board. Andrew (our son) and Mark (his father) were the ones waiting for you at the hotel in Washington, DC. It meant a lot to Andrew. He said your really nice (he said you said 'no worries dude'). He'll never forget it!!

Mark and Andie

Dear Mark and Andie,

I am delighted to learn that saying something as superficial as 'no worries dude' can leave people convinced that I'm a great chap. Things have generally picked up for me since I started saying that instead of 'piss off and leave me alone'. (Which is what I'm really thinking.)

TH

FACT: Since 2007, skateboarding sales have dropped by 2 per cent every year.

SO WE'RE HEADING IN THE RIGHT DIRECTION.

Hey Tony,

I just wanted to say you and your son were awesome today at the Tony Hawks boom boom huck jam!

Good luck to you and your son by the way, I hope your son grows up to be pro like you!

You better watch your son cause all the girls might go for him he is a cutie but too young for me!!!

Always Jessy 14 years old!

PS – I've always been a big fan to you and always will cause I wish I was as good as you!!! Is a flip a good board to start out with?

Dear Always Jessy,

Good name, and so much better than 'All ways Jessy', which has unsavoury connotations. Thank you for the kind words about me and my son. I have to confess I was unaware that I had any male offspring, but there you go – you learn something every day.

Look forward to meeting you at the next 'Tony Hawks Boom Boom Huck Jam'. These are proving very popular and they are a lot of fun to host. I'm particularly pleased to see that this time around home-made marmalade sales were up on last year's event.

TH

'Go on, you can do it!'

'Go on, you can do it!'

It is important to encourage children, particularly young boys, to take on challenges that are a little beyond them. With some carefully chosen words – I've always found 'Go on, you can do it!' to be just the job – soon the boy will be taking on something he really shouldn't, and you can simply continue on your way quickly and avoid becoming embroiled in any consequences.

hey man ur a gr8 sk8r u real cool u know u da best eva i wanna b like u

paul

Paul

I don't think you do want to be like me – because if you were like me, you'd be irritated by people who write sk8r instead of skater. It doesn't really save any time and it's ugly on the eye.

See you l8r.

TH

FACT: Skateboarders are getting older.[*] In 2006, 71 per cent of the group were in the 12–17 age demographic. Today only 45 per cent are 12–17.

CLEAR EVIDENCE THAT YOUNG PEOPLE AREN'T AS STUPID AS THEY LOOK.

[*] Sadly, we're all getting older. There's no way to prevent this process other than suicide. And even skateboarding is preferable to that.

Good day Tony, well more skateboarder it!

They are my favourite Tony, which weaves itself far over other higher indications such as Blair, which the strange involved one involved in this involvation, but the type of orignal you are, the Mr. Hawk best. Can you teach me as the kind, among them monospecial complete it all levels certain revolutions, without falling again to the fraud? I would like to know likewise, which good indications of a carrot hardened. Thanks in advance well at you the Mike

Dear Mike,

Stop taking drugs.

Right now.

TH

English comedian and author Tony Hawks.

History of the skateboard

The skateboard was originally invented in Denmark in 1162 – by Danes, surprisingly enough. Mainly they used it for moving herring around the place but they stopped doing this around 1164 when they realised there was little point in moving herring around the place. The skateboard then seems to have been forgotten about until the Enlightenment in Europe when Voltaire used one to escape persecution from the French king Louis (I'm not sure which number but definitely between one and eighteen), who despised Voltaire because of his seditious writing and especially flouncy hair.

Voltaire fled to London where he used his skateboard to go to meetings, and he even opened a skateboard park in Bow. (Now an ALDI supermarket.) Eventually he had his skateboard stolen and he returned to using public transport.

The skateboard again seems to have been forgotten about until it became infamous when nineteen-year-old Bosnian Serb Gavrilo Princip stood on one in Sarajevo in 1914 in order to gain a few extra inches in height, enabling him to shoot and kill the visiting Archduke Franz Ferdinand. This event set in motion a sequence of events that led to the First World War. This made the skateboard unpopular again until the year 2019, when English comedian and author Tony Hawks wrote *The A to Z of Skateboarding*, which topped the book charts in every country in the world except Ghana.

dear Tony Hawk

We are year seven students at Papamoa college my name is Tai and my partner name is Jesse. We are researching on skateboards and we think your the best person to talk to when skateboarding.

Our research question are: Who invented the skateboard and why? What are the characteristics of the skateboard and how has it changed over time? How did young people entertain them selves before 1990? How has skateboars changed our lives?

i really appreciate if the questions could be answered as soon as possible.

Yours sincerely Tai and Jesse

Tai and Jesse

Who invented the skateboard and why?
Queen Elizabeth II. To pull her lame corgis along the street.

What are the characteristics of the skateboard and how has it changed over time?
The skateboard is flat (ish) and has wheels on the bottom. Over time the paint peels off.

How has skateboars changed our lives?
It's made some of us multi-millionaires, but most just have more grazed knees than before.

How did young people entertain them selves before 1990?
Masturbation or knitting. (Sometimes both together).

TH

This is sick.

And this is something very good. The difference isn't difficult to spot. But try telling that to skateboarders.

Ignominy

Many parents have to face the ignominy of knowing that once their children have taken up skateboarding, the chances of them using a word like ignominy fall dramatically. Instead they are far more likely to say 'sick' instead of 'very good', which is both irritating and silly. Once your child starts uttering sentences like 'I'm stoked that I landed a tre-flip' you really can forget about Oxbridge as an option.

dear Tony Hawk,

I am a 15 year old high school sophmore. I want to learn how to do a kick flip. Can you give me any pointers? Thanks.

Chris

Chris

What a bugger! I just gave my last pointer away. Sweet little pup, nicest one in the litter in my opinion.

TH

FACT: Skate hardgoods sales fell 10 per cent in 2008 and were down 23 per cent in Jan/Feb 2009 combined.

SURELY THERE MUST BE A LINK BETWEEN THIS STATISTIC AND THE FACT THAT SKATE HARDGOODS ARE SHIT?

Hey Tony,

I found your wallet from about 10–15 years ago. It was in a jacket i bought from a thrift store. It has some old photos from when your children were born, when you were married, and possibly you skateboarding as a little kid? It also has some cards. Im 17 and heading off to college in a few months and i just bought a car that needs a lot of repairs, so my friends suggested i sell it. Im not sure if that is okay with you though so i wanted to check first. If its not, is it possible to meet you and return it? Chuck

Chuck

Oh dear. That woman was not my wife. How much do you want? $10,000? Name your price.

TH

Jam

It's difficult to believe, I know, but some people love skateboards so much that they make jam out of them. Not content with that, they arrange afternoons where people can come along and taste their jam.

hey tony my man,

wats up

i b staking like a mother foker yo man can you tell me how to ramp of my house bcuz i want to be real cool like your game and it is cool your game is cool. wat is it lik e to be the collest skatborder on the planet. Yo man i played your game and it is the coolist. I can grind but i bet that i kant grind like you can. what is the secret to cookin up the best olly?

your man yuppy

ZELDAdawg

Dear Ms Dawg,

I'm sorry to hear that you 'be staking like a mother foker' – this must be most distressing for you. And all that grinding? Most unfortunate.

TH (the collest skatborder on the planet)

FACT: Only 3.1 per cent of skateboards are purchased in sporting goods stores.

THE REST ARE STOLEN BY GRUBBY, DISHONEST TEENAGERS.

hi tony,
how do you grind?
Andrew, 11

Cautiously, and when no one's watching.

TH

dear tony

I playing ur game and see dat you don't look the sam in the games as you site. i tink you are hott. do yuo wear a mask? i think you are the best. i can olly and on my skat bord i can also do an olly bone-to-bone cornbread. i want to know if you can cum to howse and jump on my ramp and then we go for ice-creem and walk along the beech and wach the sun set.

irie love Billy Sixx

p,.s can u make a rollerblading game so is can play too games and not won.

Dear Billy,

If I came to your house, jumped on your ramp and then went for an ice cream and a walk along the beach to see the sunset, you have absolutely no idea how much trouble I'd get into.

TH

Kickflip

The kickflip is a manoeuvre in skateboarding in which a rider flips their skateboard 360° along the axis that extends from the nose to the tail of the deck.

But the key question is *why*? Why would you want to do that when there are so many better things to do? The page opposite offers just a few.

Hi Tony

My name is Harrison i live in England in West Sussex. I have been skating since i was 7 so thats been 3 years now . Right now i am reading you're autobiography and it's really interesting.

I try doing a kick flip but it's really hard for my. every time i try to do a kickFlip the board goes spinning forward. if you could just send me you're autograph it will be a thrilling moment for me. You're My Hero.

Harrison

Harrison

Don't try and do a kickflip in West Sussex. The air is too thin. Get your mum to drive you to East Sussex.

TH

FACT: The cost of an average pair of skateboarding shoes: $50–$100.

BUT OTHER SHOES ARE AVAILABLE. AND THEY DON'T LOOK QUITE SO SILLY.

Is it possible to kiss someone while doing a kick flip
Because that'd be radical

Brtiney

Dear Brtiney,

It is indeed possible to kiss someone while doing a kickflip although it does require a degree of good fortune. The other person has to happen to be flying through the air at exactly the same time, and in an adjacent position to you, and at pretty much the same speed. They need to be going in the same direction too, otherwise the kiss may easily turn into a butt, and precede a visit to casualty (possibly putting something of a brake on the courtship).

However, I encourage experimentation in this area. If me and my missus hadn't engaged in this kind of activity then we wouldn't have had three children or been arrested anywhere near as much.

TH

Love ♥

If you are unfortunate, you may stumble upon someone who is wearing one of these.

If you do, then try to stumble in such a way that you can contrive to rip the T-shirt as you fall.

It is difficult to believe, I know, but some people love their skateboards so much that they even buy T-shirts that inform the world about their dysfunctional personalities. Generally speaking I am against any T-shirt that has 'I ♥' instead of 'I love'. Love is not a long word to type or write and therefore should be written out in full. The heart, on the other hand, is a messy organ covered in blood which can malfunction, in which case it can make life particularly difficult, or even impossible.

I've just measured the time involved, and I can actually type 'love' much more quickly than I can source the ♥ icon on my computer. On the next page is a table which will help you to understand.

Time spent typing l-o-v-e	0.5 seconds
Time spent sourcing the ♥ symbol	15 minutes

A further point needs to be made here. 'Loving' a skateboard is a silly thing to do. In case you are in some doubt about what you should love, I have compiled two short lists that will clarify things for you in this area.

THINGS THAT ARE OK TO LOVE

1. Your mum and dad.
2. That man/woman who waits at the bus stop.
3. Gloves.
4. Tony Hawks.
5. Fish.
6. Toast.

THINGS THAT ARE *NOT* OK TO LOVE

1. Skateboards.
2. New York.
3. Manchester United.
4. Tony Hawk.
5. The back catalogue of Chris de Burgh.
6. Loud sirens.

Dear Mr. Tony,

Although I know that you do not know me, I hope you although want to help me.

Due to various causes (heart and stroke which I am well recovered), I am financially in trouble. Therefore I hope for the generosity of you to help me or I will lose my home. So far no one has wanted to help me, not nationally nor internationally. I hope that you can and will help me.

It concerns the mortgage of €390,000 and a loan of €190,000. I would ask you to invest in me the total amount of € 580,000 so I can get my life back on track. I will not only be very grateful, but the first period for a minimum of 10 years I'll pay an amount of €1,500 per month back.

If you want to help me partly, to cushion the worst problems you could help me with a sum of €90,000. I will pay you €300 in this case per month back. I hope you will help me as soon as possible, otherwise I will lose my house and everything around it.

FACT: A skate shop owner operating a store that sells $475,000 worth of goods might only net about $30,000 in profit.

ALL THE MORE REASON FOR THEM TO GIVE IT UP AND GET A PROPER JOB – LIKE SOLICITOR, QUANTITY SURVEYOR, OR COMEDIAN AND AUTHOR.

I hope as soon as possible for a hopefully, please before July 10, 2016, positive response. If you have any questions or comments then I am of course respond as soon as possible.

A copy of my pay slip and ID I will submits to show you that I am desperate.

Yours sincerely, Lucien

My dear Lucien,

How kind of you to write. Naturally I am always open to letters of this nature and in this case I am particularly impressed by the way in which you outline your position. You are, as you succinctly point out, 'in financial trouble'. You are quite right to assume that potential helpers like me aren't remotely interested as to how you arrived in such a state or indeed, whether you have any moral virtues that might make you an appealing person to assist. No, this sort of information doesn't interest us in the slightest. All we want to know is how much you want off us and when. (Sending a payslip also helps. Actually, to be honest, the payslip was the clincher – well done for including that.)

You'll find that all the money you need will be in your account by Thursday lunchtime unless something unthinkable happens like me returning to my senses.

Regards

TH

£64 worth of cheese.

Money

Difficult though it may be to believe, skateboards cost money. They are made of wood, and wood doesn't grow on trees. Cheap ones are available for around £25, and the most expensive models that are made of gold and encrusted with diamonds cost over £100. Now, I'm no mathematician, but by my calculations that makes the average cost of a skateboard £64.

Here is a list of things you can buy for £64 which, in my view, constitute money much better spent.

THINGS YOU CAN BUY FOR £64

£64 worth of potatoes
£64 worth of cheese
£64 worth of apples
£64 in Boots gift vouchers
An antique walking stick

hi

tony my names william i was wandering if you could find me some cheats for 'Tony Hawks pro skater 3' because i have tried some websites and i cant find any that work so if you can do that I'll be ever so grateful thanks

WILLIAM

William

The best 'cheat' is to go to a store, find *Pro Skater 3* and then leave the shop without paying for it. If they catch you, just say that I said it was OK.

TH

PS. Remember that prison life can be hard.

FACT: An Internet store might make $100,000 per year greater profit than a physical retail store with comparable sales.

THIS IS BECAUSE MOST SKATEBOARDERS ARE COMPUTER LITERATE BUT STRUGGLE WITH COMPLEX SENTENCES LIKE 'WHERE'S THE SKATEBOARD SHOP?'

hey tony you rock your one of my faviorute people you are the worlds best skater when i grow up i want to be a pro skater as well i can kick flip i can heel flip i can ollie thirty centermeters i am the best skater in my class and yesterday i landed a melon see you later bye

(P.S.please write back)

You landed a melon?
Was it still edible afterwards?

TH

what is the best skate
Alesh in Slovenia

Alesh

Skates are cartilaginous fish belonging to the family Rajidae in the superorder Batoidea of rays. More than 200 species have been described, in thirty genera. The two subfamilies are Rajinae (hardnose skates) and Arhynchobatinae (softnose skates).

As for which one is the best? Fuck knows.

TH

National No Skateboarding Day

In 2017 I introduced National No Skateboarding Day amidst a blaze of indifference. After much discussion (between myself and my neighbour and fellow committee member) we decided on 5 June. On this day, we urge everyone to encourage skateboarders to lay down their boards and devote their days to considering the futility of their pastime. Eventually, when we have attracted more funding, we will lay on spelling and grammar lessons and teach young skateboarders not to write sentences like 'U R GR8', or take similar liberties with the English language.

The movement continues to flourish, with an impressive growth in the number of those who have laid down their skateboards and respected a 'wheels-free' day, from six people in 2017 to something in the region of thirteen people in 2019.

However, we are not complacent and we continue to work hard to ensure growth continues.

So I just started out skateboarding and I didn't have any new shoes so I had to use my old ones... which unfortunately got mud all over my griptape... is there anyway I can clean my griptape without taking away the grip or damaging my board?

Thanks!! Jud X

Jud

I'm so glad you asked this question. Questions about mud and grip tape keep me going on those days when it feels like everything is falling apart. Like today for instance. I can't find my skateboard and I think my cat is seeing another woman. You've lifted me with your question. Thanks for that.

Oh – goodness – I nearly forgot to answer your question about whether you can clean your grip tape without taking away the grip or damaging your board. I'll answer it here: no.

TH

FACT: The most common place to ride a skateboard outside of a park: the driveway.

IT'S ALSO THE BEST WAY TO ANNOY THE NEIGHBOURS AND FLAG UP TO YOUR PARENTS THAT YOU'RE NOT DOING YOUR HOMEWORK.

TONY & CREW; Please take a minute!!! I am trying to contact you for a 4rth grader that has a science project due in just a couple days!!! He is in danger of failing the 4rth grade if he doesn't ACE this project:) His subject is 'Aerodynamics of a Skateboard' If you could help in anyway please email us @ xxxxxxx.com

Paul

Paul

Thanks for writing to me and my 'crew'. I'm not quite sure to whom you are referring when you use the word 'crew' – presumably my mother and her friends?

Either way, yes, about the aerodynamics of a skateboard. For his project, the best thing for him to do is to type the words 'aerodynamics' and 'skateboard' into Google, then copy and paste the most complicated stuff that is written there. If that doesn't get him an 'ace', then type 'life as a complete failure' into Google and see what it says then.

TH

Ollie

An 'ollie' is a thing that you do on a skateboard, and as such is to be avoided. If you come across an 'ollie' or inadvertently find yourself 'doing one', then contact the emergency services immediately.

Ollie is also the name of a little boy who lives in Plymouth who is sensible enough not to do skateboarding. Here is a picture of Ollie enjoying some downtime with the book *Essential Grammar*.

Hi Tony I am 13 year old boy from a small town in England in north Yorkshire and we are in need of a skatepark. I would be so happy if you could help the bored kids in Settle (our town) however you could. Ollie

Hi Ollie

How apt that you have been named after a skateboard trick. My two boys – 900 and Kickflip – feel you got a better deal than them.

Can I ask why the kids are bored in your town? I find it very difficult to believe that a small town in North Yorkshire could be dull.

TH

FACT: In 2006, more than 10 million people in the United States said that they were skateboarders.

TEN YEARS LATER 62,984,825 OF THEM VOTED FOR TRUMP. I TELL YOU: THEY'RE BONKERS.

I just wancha tell u that eye think ur an awsome sk8tr but that ur pic on ur websight don't look lik u do in ur game. Ur look way 2 old n u dont have enuf polys.

+, ur SQL code's borken, #36 n #37 r the same, as is #76 n #77

hasta
'Mickey-P' Staker

Hiya Mickey P

I can assure you my SQL code is not borken – or even broken. I just checked number 37 and it was functioning fine. OK, it needed a little oil, but that was all.

Furthermore, I do have enough polys. I have seven. Surely that's enough? One for every day of the week.

TH

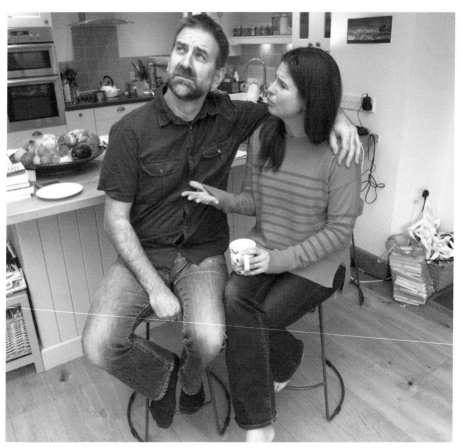

A couple attempting to process the news that their child has just been spotted skateboarding in the local park.

Parents' pain

Pain is what is experienced by all parents when they discover that their child wants to skateboard. The parents' only recompense is the pain their child feels when they fall off their skateboard. However, whatever happens to the child, it will never match the pain a parent feels when they suddenly realise that all those sleepless nights, sacrifices and the decimation of their sex life have simply produced a layabout who will say, 'That's rad,' instead of, 'That's first-class.'

Shoot me a friend request! Nik

Nik

Fuck. This is the fifth time I've done this. Instead of shooting you a friend request, I've gone and shot your friend. The one with the long hair and the knee pads. Sorry about that. Fortunately, I didn't kill him but I doubt he'll be skateboarding for a while.

TH

FACT: The United States accounts for more than 50 per cent of the total skateboarding market.

AND THAT MARKET IS ON THE FIRST SUNDAY OF EVERY MONTH. UNLESS IT'S RAINING.

I am currently doing my NCS and we are trying to hold a skate day to raise money for the Dame Kelly Holmes Trust. We wondered whether you could help us in anyway possible by donating a raffle prize or...??

I look forward to hearing from you.

kind regards

Charlie

Dear Charlie,

How is the NCS (Nude Canoeing Scheme) going? These government schemes are very good and the nude canoeing is one of the better ones. Good luck with the fundraising day. I can donate the slender briefs I wore when I did my NCS. I'll pop them in the post. (Sorry about the stain.)

TH

Quorn

This is the only other thing I can think of that is as pointless as a skateboard.

hello, I am a kid living in Ontario, NY and I am 13 years old. i am doing a school project where I have to be somebody else and I chose u and I wanted to do something special so I wanted to see if you, Tony Hawk, could come to my school and present with me and surprise everybody.

Preston

Preston

I can't tell you how tempting this is.

TH

FACT: Electric skateboards are actually water-resistant.

WHICH MAKES UNDERWATER SKATEBOARDING THAT MUCH SAFER. AND UNDERWATER SKATEBOARDING IS THE BEST KIND OF SKATEBOARDING BECAUSE THE REST OF US CAN'T SEE OR HEAR THE SKATEBOARDERS, AND, IN TURN, THEY DON'T GET A GRAZED KNEE WHEN THEY FALL OFF. IT'S A WIN/WIN.

Allow me to introduce myself. My name is Regina and I am a current member of the LOUD'S organization committee for 2015.

LOUD is a Leadership Congress focused in teenagers, as well as in public in general, with the only purpose to cause a positive impact in the assistants, in order to encourage them to become leaders in their society. Year after year, LOUD is organized by students with a nonprofit goal, but a social interest.

The reason of this letter is to invite Mr. Tony Hawk to participate in this year's congress as a speaker. The Congress is scheduled for the 10 and 11 of October 2015. We would love to have him participating because we consider him an amazing leader, who has served as an important agent of change in society. We would be more than honored to have him joining the congress as a speaker to share her experience.

I look forward to hearing back from you,

Regina

Sure, Regina, happy to help. Here's my rider.

2 crates of beer
4 bottles of brandy
A case of vintage wine
2 crates of cider
A jeroboam of anything (I've lost all sense of taste by this stage)
18 sick bags

Recession

During an economic recession, the first thing that people cut down on is skateboards. This is why an economic recession is actually a good thing.

Hello I hope you get this and are well. My five year old son has just started playing xbox tony hawks games and this has been followed by googling you. He thinks you are amazing I hope you receive this email and picture attached ok.

Take care mum of Tommy age 5 from kent England.

Dear Mum of Tommy,

Yep. Got the picture of you and Tommy. You both look very nice. Especially you.
You don't happen to be free for dinner next week by any chance?

TH

FACT: 500. That's the total number of skateboarding parks that exist in the United States right now.

500. THAT'S THE TOTAL NUMBER THAT NEED TO BE REMOVED AND REPLACED WITH AREAS FOR QUIET READING.

HI TONY WAT UP?

ME AND MY M8 JAMES FINK U R A GR8 SKATER AND SUMDAY WE WANT TO BE LIKE U. WE R THE VEST SK8ERS AROUND. MY NAME IS ANDY. PLZ WRITE BAK

Andy

What do you mean when you say 'WE R THE VEST SK8ERS AROUND'? What is a vest skater? Is it cool to skate in a vest?

Think again.

TH

hola soy un skater y soy de cantabria y tenmos nuestro grupo de skaters cntx rapido

Who are you calling a 'cntx'? How rude. I do my best, you know.

TH

Stun

Young skateboarders are quite easy to stun. My favourite way of doing this is by booking myself in as a special guest at a skateboard park, and then reading from one of my books. As you can see from this photo, it never fails to disappoint.

ALL UR GAMES ARE COOL. AND I CANT WAIT FOR THE THE NEW TONY HAWKS 5 GAME T.H.U.G. AS SOON AS IT COMES OUT IM GETTIN IT FOR DEFFINENT!!!!!!!!.

Hello there,

Glad to hear that you are going to get the T.H.U.G. game. I am very proud of it. I am also pleased that you are going to get it for Deffinent. Deffinent is a nice lad, and people very rarely get him presents. Well done.

TH

FACT: It wasn't always called skateboarding. When it first gained in popularity, skateboarding was initially called 'sidewalk surfing'. This was because skaters would replicate the techniques of surfers, but on a paved surface.

HOW STUPID IS THAT? SURFING A WAVE IS STUPID ENOUGH (WERE THESE THRILL-SEEKERS NEVER INTRODUCED TO BEDROOM SLIPPERS AS YOUNGSTERS?) – BUT DOING IT ON A PAVEMENT?! THE ONLY UPSIDE WOULD BE THAT IT WOULD BE QUICKER TO GET THEIR HEADS EXAMINED AFTER THEY'D OPENED THEM UP ON THE CONCRETE.

hoi ik vind je cooll schijf terug

Thank you very much indeed. I agree, it is impressive – although I didn't realise it was so visible in the Lycra shorts.

TH

hey tony hawk like to say your the best my skate broad got broken when i was grinding on a pole could u send me a extra broad

cody

Cody

If there are any extra broads going, then I shall keep them to myself.

TH

PS. I suspect that your grinding on a Pole caused him a great deal of discomfort and probably made him greatly miss Warsaw.

Tony Hawk

Tony Hawk (27 October 1914–9 November 1953) was a Welsh poet and writer whose works include the poems 'Do not go gentle into that good night' and 'And death shall have no dominion'; the 'play for voices' *Under Milk Wood*; and stories and radio broadcasts such as *Portrait of the Artist as a Young Dog* and *A Child's Christmas in Wales*. He became widely popular in his lifetime and remained so after his premature death at the age of thirty-nine in New York City. By then he had acquired a reputation, which he had encouraged, as a 'roistering, drunken and doomed poet'.

How long did it take to land the 900?

mr.me

Mr. You

Ages. Air traffic control made me circle Heathrow for forty minutes.

TH

FACT: Only 40 per cent of skateboarders actually wear the appropriate gear when they ride.

THERE USED TO BE A SIMILAR PROBLEM, EVEN WITH SENSIBLE ORDINARY PEOPLE – THEY JUST WOULDN'T WEAR SEAT BELTS IN CARS. HOWEVER, WHEN WE MADE THEM COMPULSORY, THEY DID. WE SHOULD DO THE SAME WITH SKATEBOARDING AND MAKE IT COMPULSORY TO WEAR THE APPROPRIATE GEAR. THAT WOULD ESTABLISH AN IMPORTANT PRECEDENT. THEN WE COULD GET ON WITH THE BUSINESS OF BANNING IT ALTOGETHER.

Dear Tony

I think you are cool, and my sister does too. Would you teach me some tricks? I really want to become a good skateboarder. How do you make a half-pipe? How old were you when you started skateing? How old were you when you learned how to do a kick flip? Do you ever come to Meigs County, Ohio to a skate park called Skatetopia? If so, would you let me know the next time you plan on being there.

Your biggest fan,

DiJaun

DiJaun

My, what a lot of questions. For answers, see below.

Q: Would you teach me some tricks? A: No
Q: How do you make a half-pipe? A: Take a whole pipe and cut it down the middle.
Q: How old were you when you started skateing? A: None of your business.
Q: How old were you when you learned how to do a kick flip? A: I'm not telling you.
Q: Do you ever come to Meigs County, Ohio to a skate park called Skatetopia? A: No.
Q: If so, would you let me know the next time you plan on being there. A: You can rest assured, I shan't be there.

Now, there you are. Still like me? I doubt it.

TH

Gandhi relaxing on a skateboard.

Underachievement

Many activities lead to underachievement, but none can hold a torch to skateboarding. To illustrate my point, below I have compiled a list of great achievers, detailing how many hours they spent skateboarding as children.

ARISTOTLE — 0 hours
LEONARDO DA VINCI — 0 hours
GANDHI — ½ hour
WINSTON CHURCHILL — 45 minutes
DONALD TRUMP — 56,895 hours

Tony what was your first ever trick you did and what was your favourite trick you ever did?

Liam

Liam

I've stopped turning tricks since they cleaned things up around King's Cross.

You probably wouldn't want to know what the trick was.

TH

FACT: Norway didn't like skateboarding. From 1978 to 1989, Norway banned skateboarding because of the high number of skateboarding accidents. Importing skateboards, selling skateboards and even owning one was punishable by a fine.

I LOVE NORWAY! BUT WHY DID THEY WEAKEN IN 1989? OK, THAT WAS THE YEAR THE BERLIN WALL FELL AND VAST NUMBERS OF EUROPEANS WERE ABLE TO ENJOY NEW FREEDOMS. BUT THE NORWEGIANS REALLY SHOULD HAVE KEPT ON SUPPRESSING THE SKATEBOARDERS.

I am called ralphy I am 12 years old. Would you tell me how to do a vairl flip.

Ralphy

What a fab name. More people should be called Ralphy in my view. But not so many that it becomes really confusing. (One in eight would be more than enough.)

Re. the vairl flip; here's what to do.

1) Lean forward holding the egg in your left hand.
2) Recite the poem at considerable volume.
3) Lean back.
4) Throw up.
5) Apologise to those around you.

It's always worked for me.

TH

The nine cardinals who competed in the 2016 semi-final.

Vatican

The Vatican needed eleven skateboarders to compete in the Inter-Faith World Skateboarding Championship semi-finals in 2016. They were firm favourites to beat the Church of Jesus Christ of Latter-Day Saints but just before kick-off (or kickflip-off as it is more accurately known), two cardinals were stuck listening to long skateboarding stories in confession and missed the semi-final completely. Being two cardinals short proved crucial and the Church of Jesus Christ of Latter-Day Saints went on to win by 5 ollies to 4 (after extra time). Pope Ollie IV was said to be devastated. Seven years later, he was dead.

94

Bout ye big guy!!!!! Tone, I'm like ur biggest fan. i'm 9yrs old and bin sk8ing for like 2 years ur amazing man, u rock dude i am your biggestt fan i gotta go luv will

Will

We should hook up some time. You seem exactly my type of guy. It would be nice to sit down over a sherry and discuss Proust, listen to poetry and do the odd 'ollie' if the fancy takes us. I'll be in touch.

Possibly.

TH

FACT: The first official skateboarding competition was held in California in 1965.

IT WAS ABANDONED SHORTLY AFTERWARDS WHEN SOMEONE REALISED THAT BECAUSE THEY HAD NO GOALS OR BALLS, THERE WAS ABSOLUTELY NO WAY OF WORKING OUT WHO HAD SCORED, AND THEREFORE WHO HAD WON OR LOST.

THE FOLLOWING YEAR ENGLAND WON THE WORLD CUP. IT WAS EASY TO WORK OUT WHO HAD WON BECAUSE THE ENGLISH SCORED FOUR GOALS AND THE GERMANS ONLY TWO.

hey Tony

I' a beginner at sk8ing and I was wondering if you can send me a deck of one of yours because all of my friends say that all of the boards that I like 'they suck' but if I can get a board from you they will say it won't suck because you are my anti-drug!!

Jacob

Jacob

I like the sound of you so I'm going to send you a deck in the post. It's one I recently dismantled while on a cruise around the Caribbean on the *Britannia*.

I'm afraid I cannot accept that I am your 'anti-drug'. I'm not even your Auntie Doug. (She was a funny woman.)

TH

You suck poo

I do not. Call me old-fashioned but I suck the occasional sweet and leave it at that.

TH

Me with a group of young delinquents who have absolutely no prospect of work.

Work

Work is something that is very rarely found by young people who regularly engage in skateboarding. Here is a typical exchange that takes place at job interviews they attend:

EMPLOYER: OK, youngster, so how do you like to spend your free time?

APPLICANT: I like to go skateboarding.

EMPLOYER: (*Calling to the door*) Next please!

Although a life of drudgery in work may not be something that your average skateboarder aspires to, they need to realise that without work they probably won't have enough money to buy nice-looking shoes.

Parents need to wake up – and fast – and realise that if their children continue to skateboard, then the chance of them living a life chained to a desk will be greatly diminished.

hi tony!

cool u pleaze provide me with a crack 4 ur game? you
rule man!!!
you really rule a lot!!
gracias amigo!

Pakito.

Pakito

I would happily supply you with some crack if I could get hold of any.

TH

PS. I don't rule that much. Only in Ecuador and a small island off Denmark. (I like to think of myself as a benevolent dictator.)

FACT: According to BJS statistics, the skateboarding industry looks to stay on par with industry growth and job creation through 2020.

YES, BUT WHO TRUSTS THE BRITISH JOCKSTRAP SOCIETY? (ALTHOUGH I BELIEVE THEIR ANNUAL BALLS ARE WELL SUPPORTED.)

Dear Tony, you are my favourite skater. I went to the huckjam. It was great. I like you so much that at the huckjam I wanted to run down the stares and meat you. From Jason.

Jason

I don't let anybody 'meat me' anymore. The last time was too painful. Also, you should know that it is dangerous to 'run down the stares'. If people are staring, just let them. They'll get bored eventually and it's not big or clever to run them down.

TH

YOU ARE THE MOST ASOME SK8ER EVER!!!! SERIOUSLY YOU ROK!! DUDE I LOVE YOU!! I KNOW YOU WANT TO GO S8TING WITH ME ON SATERDAY!!!

MONKEY

Unfortunately, I have a rule not to skate with monkeys on a Saturday. I set that day aside for geese only

TH

Xmas

Some children might write to Santa thus. In a case like this, I suggest the following reply:

Dear Child,

First of all, it's not Xmas: it's Christmas. There's really no need to abbreviate a word like Christ for x's sake. Second, you should know that I don't exist. Adults have simply made me up so that you can experience huge disappointment at a later date when you find out about this deception. (Or, if you're a child reading, then right now.) Third – regarding your request for the skateboard – the answer is no. You can have something much, much cheaper that you can't fall off. Like a biro, or similar.

Yours,
Santa

waz up Tony its Connor hear i am ur number 1 fan ur the best skater in the whole wide world.i only have 1 more level on Tony Hawks American wasteland then its completed i can do a KICKFLIP and a MANUAL (P.S PLZ WRITE BACK

Hello Connor

Congratulations for all your fine achievements. Being able to do a kickflip and a manual will stand you in good stead at most job interviews, and once you get to that next level in *Tony Hawk's American Wasteland*, you will be well qualified to work in almost any wasteland.

TH

FACT: Skateboarding will officially be recognised as an Olympic sport at the 2020 Games in Tokyo.

OH MY GOD, NO.

Dear Tony, I have been skateboarding for a couple years now. I am a girl. and i am sponsered by STOKED. And i also met you when u were filming the movie the NEW GUY. but u probley dont remember me. this is a gay question but how can u get noticed for skateboarding. like how did u become so famous and get noticed and all that?

-audrey-

Audrey

I don't think this is a gay question at all. Stupid, yes, but not gay. The best way to get noticed skateboarding is to skate into other people as they walk along. It's amazing how a severe gash on people's shins can make them take notice.

TH

Hi I'am sarah

I have been skating for about a year and the boys at the skate park think i am stupid and think i should be doing dancing or something what do you think?

Sarah

Skateboard when you've mastered the apostrophe.

TH

Y bother skateboarding?

Well, come on, why? You'll only look a tit, like this.

Great to Connect with you Mr. Hawk. My name is Stefan Ramjag and I am actually not reaching out just as a fan but also to share a business project that I am launching, with you. If you can email me back I would definitely appreciate it. Thanks again, and let me know if this email address is proper to send the business plan to.

Stefan

I have always wanted to go into business with someone called Stefan Ramjag. Unfortunately, I've just put $2.5m into a joint venture with Stefan Pugjom. And the week before $600,000 with Stefan Likshag. So I'm afraid your timing is out.

TH

FACT: Jagger Eaton holds the world record for the longest rail grind at 204 feet.

NO ONE SHOULD BE RAIL GRINDING AT ALL, LET ALONE AT 204 FEET. THEY COULD EASILY COME OFF THE RAIL AND FALL ON SOMEONE'S HEAD BELOW. SOMEONE, SOMEWHERE NEEDS TO STOP THIS ALTITUDE RAIL GRINDING. DOES IT NEED AN ACT OF PARLIAMENT?

To be quite frank, I believe that you sir, are a pompous prick. Just by reading the main page of your website, I see you think very highly of yourself. I am sure that you get bombarded with emails everyday in regards to skateboarding, but to make such as a rude gesture as to respond to the fans of somebody that is not yourself... in the manner that you did, is in and out of itself, just plain assholish. I just thought you should know, I myself am a model as well, I just happen to be a skateboarder, and let me tell you one thing, you are not that striking. I would say moderately handsome at most.

– A person actually sort've offended by your 'mischievous replies'

Dear Quiet Frank,

I am deeply disturbed to have upset another male model, particularly one who is (unless I have misread your mail) more striking than me. Your remark that I am only 'moderately handsome at most' has cut me to the quick. Yesterday I didn't go out, and today I am only going to go to the shops with a bag over my head. (I will make holes for air though. Like you, I'm not stupid.)

Yours,
TH

Zeal

Finally, let us with great zeal reject skateboards and all those who ride on them.

Rafi Addlestone
Graham Alderson
Elizabeth Alway
Keeley Ambrose
Peter J. Anderson
Sholto Andrews
Chris Arlott
Ruth Ashton-Ward
Michael Atkins
David Austin
Nick Avery
Simon Axford

Chris Baggett
Nick Baker
Russell Barnes-Heath
Roger Barrett
Gerard Batt
Pete Beck
Adrian Belcher
Richard Bell
The Bendy One
Julian Benton
Tracey Benton
Elliott Berry

Jon Birkett
Phil Blackman
Paul & Martha Blaydon
Gilly Bolton
Fiona Boston
Yva Bourke
Matthew Bowers
Margaret Boynton
Paul Brannigan
Paul Brennan
Tony Bridgeman
Alice Broadribb

Paul Bromage
Angie Brown
Anne Brown
Lesley Browne
Phil Bruce-Moore
Gib Bulloch
Linda Burgess
Ann Burton
Marcus Butcher
Andrew Candler
Olivia Cannon
Sam Castell-Ward
Alison Catchlove
Sami Cawthorn
Rodney Challis
David Chantrey
Andy Checker
Paul Child
Caroline Claydon
Tom Cobbold
Mark Cockin
Richard Cohen
Robert Cole
Christopher Collingridge
Louis Constandinos
Andrew Coombs

Mark E Cooper
Katy Costello
Tim Craddock
John Crawford
Deborah Crook
Tom Cullen
Iain Davie
Glyn Davies
Pat Davison
Philip Dayton
John Delaney
Neil Denham
Pamela Dennison
Andrew Denny
Adam Devlin
Alison Diaper
Miranda Dickinson
Steve Dilworth
Geoffrey Doggrell
Maureen Dominey
Esteban Dominguez-
    Boonefaes
Anne Dooley-Keeney
Lee Dorrington
Dan Duffek
Chico Wolfie Dunn

Lisa Girlie Dunn
Clare Dunstall
Lydia Ellwood
Gill English
Jack Evans
Sarah Evans
Katie Farnworth
Gareth Fielding
Marius Finnstun
David Fletcher
Peter Forbes
Adam Fransella
Jim Fraser
Caroline Frear
Elaine & Martin
    Frost-Jennings
Graham Gaffney
Tom Galloway
Cathy Galvin
Sue Garner
Stephen Garvani
Steve Garvey
Mark Gethings
Richard Gibson
Jenni Gill
Marcus Gipps

Trudi Godfrey
Simon Goldsmith
Tracey Gonzalez
George Goodfellow
Ian Grey
Melanie Griffin
Elaine Griffiths
Phil Hall
Richard Hall
Andy Hamilton
Edward Hancox
The Lady Jan Harkin
Andrea Harms
Jamie Harris
Nicky Hartle
Monika Hartmann
Edith Hawksworth
Hans Heitmann
Wayne Hemingway
Jeff Hodges
Paul Hodges
Brian Hodgson
Claudia Hohnhorst
Debbie Holman
Helen Hood
Alison Hope

Simon Horne
Roger Houston
Steve Howe
Bob Howell
Alexander Humphries
Graham Hunt
Victoria Ichizli-Bartels
Deb Ikin
Phil Inthekitchen
Alison Irwin
Johari Ismail
Karen Jeynes
Marjorie Johns
Arwen Johnson
Alex Jones
Jason Jones
Justine Jones
Peter Jones
Nick Jordan
Clyde Kaplan
Rod Kedward
Morven Kemp
Mark Kent
Dan Kieran
Dave King
Julian King

Stephen Kinsella
Richard Kirkwood
Adam Kirtland
Kevin Knight
Kristen LahteineStep
Sean Leahy
Denise Lee
Miriam Lehman
John Lenahan
Laura Lepeltier
Joanne Lines
Claire Lipscomb
Martin Lister
Richard Lloyd
Geoff Lockett
David Long
Dave Lovering-Roddis
Marion Macdonald
Chris Mackie
Karen Macleod
Mary Mahoney
Seamus Mahoney
Catherine Makin
Nigel Grant Manley
Kelly Manning
Anit Manudhane

Dave & Anne Markham
Richard Marsh
Jessica Martin
Jo Matthews
Michael Matthias
Jack Maunders
Shaun McAlister
Brian McCloskey
Gavin Mcdaid
Alfonzo McDungeon
Clint McJam
Mark McKean
Lynda Mcnamara
Ann Marie Meaney
Janet Measom
Nick Mellish
Craig Melvin
Ruth Mepham
Andy Middleton
Daryl Millar
Ann Mills-Duggan
Ian Minshull
Rob Minter
Dr Paul Minton
John Mitchinson
Mark Montague

Kim Morgan
Nick Morris
Nigel Mumford
Myszka (Mrs Fox)
Andrew Nairn
Jon Naismith
Carlo Navato
Ali Neads
Robert Nelson
Scott Nicholas
David Nicholls
Mike, Jacqui & Jacob Nichols
Paul Ninefeldt & Tanya Jordan
Anna Nock
K.L.T. Norman
Pat O'Brien
Mark O'Neill
Karen O'Sullivan
Paul Oakley
Ewan Ogilvie
Mark Oliff
Gail Ollis
Lotus Olsson
Adam Orton
Nathan Pace
Lev Parikian

Mark Parish
Steph Parker
Ruth Patman
Robert Phillips
Shaun Phillis Phillips
Justin Pollard
Beki Pope
Lawrence Pretty
Chris Quy
Adam Radford
Rosalind Ramsay
Julian Ransom
Dan Rebellato
Marcus Redman
Stephen Reid
Des Reynolds
Chris Richmond
Andy Rickeard
Kevin Roberts
Michael Robertshaw
Andrew Robinson
Dan Robinson
Ian Robinson
Alun Roderick
Geraint Rogers
George Ronksley

Katherine Rooney
Noel Rooney
Abigail Rose
Adrian Runacres
Roy Russell
Sue Sanders
Wilf Schreiber
Oliver Schwarz
Rose Seabury
Maia Sepp
Keith Shannon
Jo Sharples
Chris & Bee Shaw
Brían Sheils
Stevie Simpson
John Skilleter
Tony Slater
Keith Sleight
Amy Smith
Chris Smith
Ray Smith
Richard Smith
Trevor Smith
Kerri J Spangaro
Justin Standen
Amelia Steenkamp

Emily Stewart
Chris Stoddart
James Stone
Martin Sullivan
Sheila Synnott
Mark Taylor
Rene-Paul Taylor
Robin Taylor
Elaine Teenan
Colin Thomas
Mike Scott Thomson
Simon Tierney-Wigg
Mr Timothy (Tim) Slater
Craig Tonks
Carla Torres
Russell Turner
Vicky Vagg
Eric van Berkel
Mark Vent
Clive Walder
Kate and Marc Wallace
Nick Walpole
Francesca Ward
Sarah Watt
Peter Wells
Andrea Westcott

Christopher White
Geoffrey White
Margaret White
Andrew and Teresa Widd
Mark Wiggin
Christine Wilhelm
Samantha Wilkinson
Paul Willgoss MBE
Arwel Williams
Craig Williams
Martin Winch
Christopher Worrall
Owen Yapp

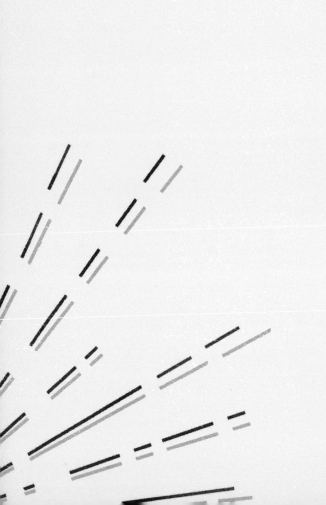